Agenda

1. **Making the Most of your Assets**
    School grounds and the Curriculum

2. **It's Child's Play**
    The importance of the Informal Curriculum

3. **Only Playing**
    Design and use of the grounds

4. **Stop Playing About**
    Management of the Informal Curriculum

5. **Play it Safe**
    Safety and maintenance

6. **Playing with Ideas**
    Making changes

Making the Most of Your Assets

School grounds and the Curriculum

It has been estimated that the 30,000 schools in the UK have over 120,000 acres of school grounds between them. In some schools the 'grounds' consist mainly of tarmac whilst others have large expanses of grass; many schools have both. Whatever size or type, your school grounds are a unique and very valuable asset.

For years the potential of school grounds has gone largely unrecognised. 'The school' has come to mean the buildings with the grounds being relegated to a kind of 'no-man's land'.

This is changing for a variety of reasons. Schools are beginning to look anew at their grounds and realise that they could provide a wonderful educational resource - right on the doorstep.

The Formal Curriculum

At least 50% of the formal or National Curriculum can be taught in school grounds. In fact 20% can best be learned outside: not only PE but Science, Maths, Technology, English, Drama and even Religious Education. Schools throughout the country are beginning to recognise this, and there are hundreds of examples of exciting and innovative ways of developing school grounds into outdoor classrooms.

The Informal Curriculum

Children may spend as much as 25% of each school day in play/breaktime, usually (weather permitting !) in the school grounds. This time is part of the school day and part of children's education, during which they will be learning, hence the term 'The Informal Curriculum'. What children learn during this time may be positive or negative, but the fact that they **are** learning whilst playing is beyond question.

● *What constitutes your school grounds ? - How much land is there - what features do the grounds contain - when did you last 'walk the bounds' of your school ?*

● *How often are your school grounds used for lessons ? Which subjects are taught there?*

● *How much time do your children spend in the 'Informal Curriculum' every day, week, term, year ?*

The Hidden Curriculum

● - What do the grounds 'say' about your school ?
- Is it a caring and welcoming place which inspires a sense of wonder, excitement and respect ?

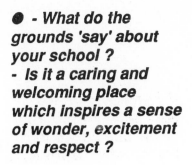

Whether or not school grounds are well used, their very existence affects and influences pupils, staff, parents and the community at large. Coming to school may involve a short walk across a tarmac playground or along a path beside the playingfield. Yours may be an 'open access school' with public rights of way. It may be surrounded by a high brick wall, low fence or railings. Pupils, staff and parents experience the space outside the school daily - school does not begin at the door to the building. The nature of this space makes a statement about your school.

Recent research has shown that the 'messages' conveyed by the nature of the school grounds - what may be called the 'Hidden Curriculum' - are very powerful.They influence both attitudes to and the management of the school in all kinds of ways.

The significance of school grounds for children

To children, school grounds are enormously significant. Children recognise the grounds, particularly the playground of their school as a unique place, somewhere created especially for them, apparently to do the things they enjoy and which are increasingly impossible elsewhere.

Children today have less freedom and independent mobility than previous generations. Parental concerns about traffic and other potential hazards and the lack of appropriate, accessible, outdoor spaces/places where children can play close to home have caused a fundamental change in childhood lifestyle.

Children therefore need school grounds and the opportunities they offer more than ever before. It is therefore essential that school grounds meet these needs effectively, for the benefit of all our children.

It's Child's Play

The importance of the Informal Curriculum

The term 'Informal Curriculum' is used here to describe both the times of the day when children are in school but not involved in lessons, i.e. break and mid-day playtime, as well as what they do at those times, i.e. play.

Provision of break and playtime should not be merely a matter of administrative convenience - a time for staff to have a 'loo and coffee break' or even, though it may be beneficial, a time for staff and children to 'have a break from each other'.

The Informal Curriculum provides opportunity for children to engage in a form of learning which is different from, but equally important as the Formal Curriculum.

Play matters

Play is a complex subject. Perhaps because of this the significance of play is sometimes not fully understood. It is confused with amusement, diversion, 'letting off steam', thought to be 'a waste of time'. Nothing could be further from the truth !

Play is the means by which we learn without being taught. For this reason it is often described as 'Nature's way of learning'. The need to learn, to understand ourselves, other people, places and things, is essential to healthy human development. This need finds its natural outlet through play. Indeed, much that is learned through play cannot be learned any other way.

Play is a process. It is the process of doing, exploring, discovering, failing and succeeding. It is not the outcome or end result. Play takes many forms. It is sometimes described as having various functions because it serves a variety of different developmental needs.

● *Why do you have play/playtime in your school ?*

● *What are the aims and objectives of the 'Informal Curriculum' in your school ?*

● *How does the Informal Curriculum provide for these play needs of children in your school?*

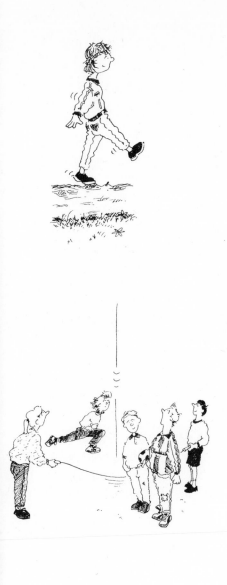

Play and physical development

For children, the desire to run, jump, crawl, climb and swing is natural and, given the chance, these physical activities will form part of their play. Research shows that such activities improve co-ordination skill, bone and muscle growth, strength, agility and endurance - all of which are essential to the developing child but also, in the long term, to health in later life.

Play and social development

Play enables social and emotional development. Children need to play with others to experience and understand about tolerance, co-operation and sharing, and the importance of respecting the views, feelings and opinions of others.The acquisition of social skills is essential to normal growth and development.

Play and cognitive development

Through play children discover, explore and develop an understanding of the environment around them and the world in which they live. Places need to be explored to be understood, known to be valued, familiar to inspire a sense of security. Children need to discover the cause/effect relationship between the environment and their own behaviour if they are to develop into responsible and caring citizens.

Children can, or should, be able to play without being organised by adults. But, children need adults to **enable** play. Positive play experiences cannot happen in a vacuum however ingenious and creative children may be. Children need time to play, access to environments of quality to play in and other people to play with. They need adults to provide these opportunities. It is therefore essential that those involved in the management of schools have an understanding of the value and purpose of play and how to provide for it, in order to ensure that children are getting maximum benefit from the Informal Curriculum.

Only Playing
Design and use of the grounds

What children do - or are able to do - in terms of the Informal Curriculum will be largely determined by the nature or design of the grounds.

The amount of space is, in itself, a key factor and one which you are unlikely to be able to do much about ! However, it does not necessarily follow that 'big is beautiful'. The way the space is managed is also significant, but essentially the quality of the environment determines the quality of experience.

Even the most imaginative child will find it difficult to be creative and sociable in a bleak, barren, sterile space for a quarter of every school day. At best, such spaces are breeding grounds for boredom and unhappiness. At worst they may actually cause hostility, bullying and an ethos of 'survival of the fittest'.

The grounds should provide for all aspects of the Informal Curriculum, at least to some degree. Children need space; things to play with and on; places in which to socialise with others as well as places to 'get away' from others and be alone.

In terms of the Informal Curriculum, children need environments which offer potentiality, diversity, flexibility and opportunity for interaction. Where the range of options is limited, then obviously the quality of the Informal Curriculum will be limited and childrens' experience will be imbalanced and incomplete. In short the grounds should, by design, support the aims and objectives of the Informal Curriculum.

Use of space

Analysis of the way the grounds are used by children will help to identify the ways in which the design or nature of the space is influencing use. Patterns of activity may have developed in certain locations, either by tradition or by some groups claiming territorial rights, and this may not result in the most effective use of the space.

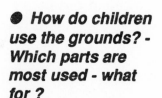

● *How do children use the grounds? - Which parts are most used - what for ?*

● *Are 'out of bounds' areas really necessary - could other ways be found to overcome design problems ?*

Equally, management decisions will affect use of the space. Some schools have large grassy areas which are frequently 'out of bounds', forcing all children onto small areas of tarmac causing serious congestion.

Lack of space or poor design may be alleviated by 'zoning' areas by activity or age. Research suggests that segregation by age may remove the need to 'take care of the little ones' and increase the degree of aggressive play amongst older ones. Also many children, particularly girls, derive great pleasure from playing with younger ones. The opportunity to mix with those of a different age, to learn to take account of their needs, and to pass on games and skills is a positive and valuable part of the Informal Curriculum.

Zoning by activity may be preferable. However, labelling of particular areas for certain activities is pointless unless the space actually supports the given purpose - or is made to do so. For example, it is not sufficient to allocate that part of the grounds currently least used because it receives little sunlight, is totally featureless and inherently least attractive as a 'quiet area' and expect it to be popular. Of course, if it becomes popular it is unlikely to remain quiet for long !

Football is a common concern. Some schools really do have too little space to permit the playing of games involving large numbers of children - particularly when 'missiles' of any description are used - but these are rare. Before banning this, or any other game, it is worth considering whether a particular area can be set aside, remembering that children can and will adapt games to the amount of space available - however large or small!

Things to play with, on and under

To children, everything in the grounds offers potential as a play object, whether intended for the purpose or not, at least until they have been sufficiently explored and investigated!

In order to fulfil their need for physical activities, children will seek out objects to climb, swing, slide and jump on. This need diminishes with age, but such activities are a fundamental part of childhood, not only for infants but throughout the primary school years. If opportunities are not provided, children will utilise anything available, such as walls, fences, drainpipes, flower beds, dustbins and even each other!

● *What do your grounds offer in terms of things to play with and on - which aspects of the Informal Curriculum do these support ?*

Fixed play equipment may help in meeting this need. However, much of this type of equipment was designed originally for use in park playgrounds and is not necessarily appropriate for use in school grounds.

Markings for games such as hopscotch are common features of grounds, but schools often report that these are little used. This may be due to a lack of interest in, or knowledge of the type of play which the markings are intended to support; they may be badly sited, e.g. on a pathway, making play difficult; or children may be bored with them. Where markings have been designed by children, as part of a formal curriculum activity, schools report increased interest and use.

The potential of an otherwise featureless environment may be greatly enhanced by the introduction of loose or mobile equipment. Sufficient quantity of items is essential and it should be accepted from the outset that some degree of loss or damage is inevitable as such equipment it likely to be heavily used.

The comfort factor

The majority of school grounds are uncomfortable places. Whilst children rarely need to sit down because they are tired it can be almost impossible for them to find a quiet place to sit and talk, share a joke or secret fear.

Seats, if provided, are usually found either on the edge of the football area or some other exposed location, forcing children who do not want to run around, to stand huddled in groups against the building, or sit on steps in doorways.

The degree of comfort - or discomfort is also greatly affected by shade and shelter or the lack of them. Wide open spaces without wind breaks are, according to most teachers, guaranteed to produce problems in terms of children's behaviour. Equally, where children are forced to spend an hour or so in a tarmacced suntrap they are likely to become uncomfortable and even unwell.

Privacy is important to children as well as adults. Whilst the concern of supervisors that they should be able to see all of the children all of the time is widespread, is it really necessary? The lack of places to 'get away to' may exacerbate problems such as bullying because children are unable to physically distance themselves from others. And, apart from anything else, hiding remains a much favoured activity amongst children !

Place not space

In addition to the basic elements of space and 'things to do', there are other less specific but equally important considerations in terms of the design of the grounds. School grounds should, by design, enable and offer the potential for all aspects of the Informal Curriculum, not just games and physical activities - places to read, make up stories and act out plays, marvel at the antics of a spider, delight in the properties of soil and generally to ponder the wonders of the universe.

● *Would you spend time in your school grounds if you didn't have to?*

In addition to the functional uses the grounds need to support, they should be special places which children delight in and value because they posses a 'sense of place'. It is essential that grounds offer diversity, flexibility and change; stimulate the senses through variety of colour, texture, shapes; provide a stimulating and exciting 'place to be', which is reflective of and responsive to children's needs.

Stop Playing About
Management of the Informal Curriculum

The management of the Informal Curriculum has recently received increased attention as a result of concern about bullying and other behavioural problems arising during or as a result of playtime. There may be many causes of such problems, including the nature of the environment itself, and it is obviously necessary to identify the causes before solutions can be found.

Whether or not your school is aware of such problems, the way the Informal Curriculum is managed merits consideration.

In most schools, morning and afternoon breaktime is supervised by teaching staff and the mid-day break by supervisors. Supervisors usually have a dual role: to organise the eating of lunch inside the building and then to supervise playtime. This in itself creates problems because the two jobs are quite different. Equally, whilst the ratio of supervisors to children may be adequate inside the building, it maybe insufficient during playtime when children are moving around a large open space. This sometimes leads to the introduction of rules to restrict the amount of space used for play which in turn creates further problems.

Status and kudos is very significant. Children recognise this, particularly by the sanctions supervisors are able - or unable - to impose. Also, where play is accorded little importance, the adults responsible for playtime may come to be viewed as being somehow inferior. Even apparently insignificant matters, such as the wearing of overalls when doing playground duty, conveys messages to children. And of course, some children will exploit such situations.

Lack of involvement in the overall management of the school can lead to supervisors feeling and being ancillary, and to a sense of powerlessness when faced with difficulties.

● *Has the job description of supervisors been reviewed recently ?*

● *What kinds of problems do supervisors experience?*

Supervisors who are relegated to performing the role of policing the playground, who through lack of training and skill, are unaware that the manner in which they address children will determine the manner of response, and who have nothing to 'give' in terms of skills, are condemning the children, themselves and everyone else to a daily diet of frustration.

● What skills and abilities are required by those who manage the Informal Curriculum ?

Having identified the aims and objectives of the Informal Curriculum it is important to consider the role of those responsible for supervising or managing it. This will probably produce a lengthy list of skills, attributes and tasks - friend and confidant, referee, collector of 'strays', guardian, source of endless ideas, provider of useful supplies, comforter etc. Not to mention the ability to watch over a large number of moving bodies even when they are behind you!

Ideally, the role is that of facilitator. The business of facilitating play is complex and requires considerable ability. Some folk may posses natural ability to perform this role. However, most people will need help to do the job well.

● Have the supervisors in your school attended any training ? - which aspects of their work would benefit?

Formal training may be available via the Education Authority or some other source. If resources can be found, such opportunities should, wherever possible, be utilised. Training in First-Aid is most important, not only in terms of the well-being of the children, but also because it will enhance the confidence of supervisors who are often extremely concerned about this issue.

Schools may be able to implement 'in service' training of their own. Much can be learned by example - perhaps a rota of teachers could be organised over a given period of time so that they could work with the supervisors during lunchtime.

Playtime should be an enjoyable and valuable experience for children and for adults as well! A greater understanding and awareness of the purpose and value of the Informal Curriculum, shared by the teaching and non-teaching staff, may bring improvements, not only during lunchtime but throughout the school day for all concerned.

Play It Safe
Safety and maintenance

All schools will have established procedures in relation to safety and maintenance generally, and will be guided by both legislative requirements and procedures laid down by the Local Education Authority. It is obviously essential that all those involved in the management of the school are aware of such requirements and procedures. However, there are a number of issues in relation to use of the grounds for the Informal Curriculum which may merit further consideration.

Children and play

First, it must be acknowledged that there is no such thing as a completely safe play environment because there is no such thing as a safe child! Children will have accidents wherever they are - they will fall over each other, their feet and even over nothing at all!

Secondly it must be accepted that during play, children will seek challenges which offer opportunities to test competence and master new skills. This inherently involves an element of risk. They will attempt to run faster, climb higher, jump further and generally develop an understanding of their own capabilities and those of other people and things.

DANGER - BORE

These needs can and should be met. For example, opportunities to climb do not have to involve great height and can, by careful design, be provided without the need for expensive equipment and special surfacing.

Where children's play needs are not adequately provided for they will attempt to create opportunities out of boredom and frustration. In doing so they may, as a result of a lack of understanding of risk, put themselves and others in danger. Helping children to understand the consequences of play behaviour and the nature of risk may improve their personal safety and also behaviour in and use of the grounds generally.

The design of the grounds

The grounds of many schools are open access sites. Some have no boundary fencing and others contain public rights of way. Such situations may present a multitude of problems in terms of safety, care and maintenance, not only of the grounds but also of the children. There may be little or nothing which can be done to change such situations but the problems and their ramifications should be identified and carefully considered.

Maintenance and other procedures

It is obviously not possible to ensure that accidents will never happen but it is essential that those responsible for the management of schools are able to demonstrate that they have taken due care, so far as is reasonably practicable, to prevent accidents occurring.

In order to fulfill this duty of care, it is may be helpful to undertake a detailed appraisal of the grounds and the way they are used during the Informal Curriculum.

Any school with fixed play equipment in the grounds should have it regularly inspected. The Local Authority will advise.

However, because children will use everything and anything during play, including items or features not intended for this purpose, it is advisable to include these in the appraisal.

Whilst any element which constitutes a danger should be eliminated, it does not necessarily follow that use of features not intended for play constitutes a danger - though their use as play objects may not be appropriate for other reasons!

School grounds suffer very heavy use and it is therefore inevitable that signs of wear and tear will recur repeatedly. It is essential that this is noted and repaired as quickly as possible. It can be helpful if all those who use the grounds regularly, including of course the children, are aware of the need to report such damage and know the procedure for doing so.

HILDREN AT PLAY

Playing with Ideas
Making changes

Hopefully, having reached this stage, you will be convinced of the value and importance of the Informal Curriculum and of your school grounds. You may also have decided that some changes are necessary.

Throughout this booklet we have identified some important issues which need to be considered. However advice from schools which have embarked on change to improve the Informal Curriculum suggests that the process of change is almost as valuable as the outcome. It is therefore essential to take time initially to consider this process carefully to ensure the best results.

Gather information

The more information you have the better the outcome will be. Consultation with children is essential. It is important to focus on what children would like to **do**, rather than what they would like to **have** - there is a big difference. This approach will also help to avoid unrealistic expectations.

Remember to involve the adult school community in the consultation process - it's their school too! There may also be value in extending the exercise to the wider community, particularly if the school or the grounds are used by other groups.

The value of consultation cannot be over emphasised. Not only will it provide a good basis on which to take what might be major decisions, but the process of involvement of the whole school community will have long term beneficial effects in terms of ethos and attitudes to the school.

It is also important at an early stage to ensure that you have obtained all relevant information regarding legal or other requirements, and to clarify matters on which you may need permission from the Education Authority before implementing changes. Equally, it will be useful to identify possible sources of help, advice and resources.

Clarify aims and objectives

Before any changes are made, it is essential to clarify the aims and objectives of the Informal Curriculum. It is also essential that everyone understands and supports the rationale for change. This may involve many people - not only the teaching staff but the supervisors, the caretaker and perhaps also parents. Play is a complex subject, and it may therefore be necessary to consider ways of explaining concepts and broadening understanding of the issues involved in order to ensure that any changes have widespread support.

Consider the wider implications

The grounds should provide for both the Informal and the Formal Curriculum (and not only for PE!). Any changes should therefore be considered in the light of the overall impact they will have. A detailed plan of proposals should be drawn up so that the full implications may be appreciated before any action is taken. This will avoid situations occuring where the sand pit is too small for science experiments and the relocated football area has trees planted in the corners !

Consideration could also be given to ways in which different elements of the formal curriculum provide opportunities to develop plans and proposals for the grounds. Schools have found this an excellent way of involving children in the process of change.

Take a long term perspective

Changes to the physical design of the grounds will probably have long term implications in relation to maintenance which will require organisation and resourcing. Every school should devise a long term development and management plan for the grounds which reflects the uses and functions they are required to support.

Improvements may be needed and long overdue, but considered and systematic change will be more enduring and effective than 'one-off' efforts. Ideally, school grounds should never be 'finished' but should continually evolve, grow and develop to meet the changing needs of the school and its pupils.

Consider the cost

Analysis of expenditure on the Informal Curriculum is likely to show that relatively little is spent on this element of children's education. In such cases is it really realistic to expect that positive and valuable outcomes will result? In fact, it is possible that problems resulting from the way the Informal Curriculum is currently organised may actually be costing money, albeit in 'hidden' ways.

Whilst some schools have effected major physical changes to the design of their grounds in order to enhance the quality of the Informal Curriculum - at considerable cost - others have achieved equally beneficial results at relatively little expense.

Whilst it is important not to be over ambitious or unrealistic, it is equally important that needs and opportunities are not constrained from the beginning by concern about the financial implications of change. Much can be achieved by those who are prepared to be inventive, imaginative and brave !

Involve the children

Whatever the nature of change, one element which appears to be integral to a successful outcome is that of participation. Those schools which have involved children, not only in the consultation and planning stages but also in the implementation of change, are convinced of the many benefits of such participation.

Play, playtime and school playgrounds are very important to children. In reality, children are probably more concerned about these matters than anyone else !

From our research it is clear that children enjoy being consulted about this aspect of their lives. They will certainly appreciate any changes which improve their play opportunities. Most of all they will value the chance to participate in the implementation of change, to work together with adults to enhance the quality of the school grounds and subsequently to care for the environment. But then, whose school grounds are they ?